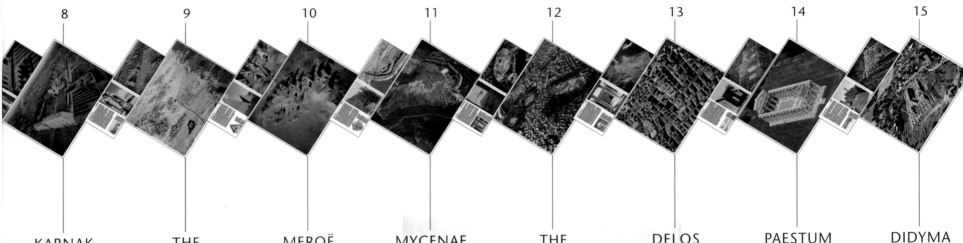

8   9   10   11   12   13   14   15

KARNAK

THE GREAT TEMPLE OF AMUN: A CITY OF PRIESTS

Egypt
Africa

c. 2000–300 BC

This is the largest temple in Egypt, dedicated to the god Amun – a city within a city, where the priests performed the rituals of the god, and an architectural feat with its pylons, courtyards, hypostyle halls, obelisks, alleys, temples and lakes.

THE RAMESSEUM

THE 'TEMPLE OF A MILLION YEARS'

Egypt
Africa

c. 1250 BC

The mortuary temple of Ramesses II at Thebes stands between the Nile and the desert. The temple was built of colossal stones, and bricks were used for the numerous outbuildings.

MEROË

THE PYRAMIDS OF SUDAN

Sudan
Africa

270 BC–AD 350

This vast cemetery of the Nubian kings was inspired by the model of the 'small' pyramids at Sheikh Abd el-Qurnah in Egypt. The pyramids feature an adjoining sanctuary, preceded by a pylon, and one or two subterranean burial chambers.

MYCENAE

THE FEUDAL AGE IN GREECE

Greece
Europe

c. 1600–1300 BC

The military and palatial architecture of the warrior Mycenaeans is reminiscent of a Homeric setting. In one of the graves, Heinrich Schliemann discovered one of archaeology's greatest treasures: the gold 'mask of Agamemnon'.

THE ACROPOLIS OF ATHENS

'THE CITY OF THE GODS'

Greece
Europe

c. 450–400 BC

The Acropolis stands on the site of an ancient fortress and boasts the most famous Greek temple on earth, the Parthenon. Between the harmony of the architecture and the perfection of its sculpture, this raised citadel is Greek art in all its beauty.

DELOS

THE ISLAND OF APOLLO IN THE HEART OF THE AEGEAN

Greece
Europe

5th century BC

When the small island of Delos became the centre of the Athenian League and the economic heart of Greece, it enjoyed tremendous prosperity. Its architecture benefited greatly: temples, agoras, religious and political buildings, and grand private residences with porticos and mosaics.

PAESTUM

TEMPLES OF MAGNA GRAECIA

Italy
Europe

6th–5th centuries BC

The Greeks founded many colonies in southern Italy, and the city of Paestum bears testament to their power and wealth. The three Doric temples found there are among the most beautiful and best-preserved examples of this ancient architecture in the world.

DIDYMA

THE ORACLE OF APOLLO IN GREEK ASIA MINOR

Turkey
Near East

4th century BC–2nd century AD

People came to the Temple of Didyma in order to consult the oracle, with priests acting as intermediaries between the individual and the prophetess. Carved in marble, the temple is remarkable for the opulence of its Hellenistic decoration.

CONTENTS

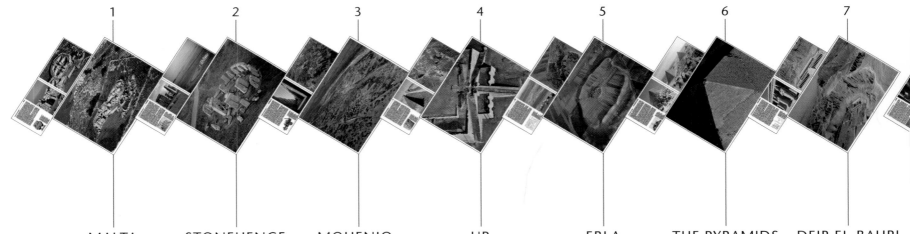

Henri Stierlin

UNFOLDING HISTORY

Thames & Hudson

'A SOLAR OBSERVATORY'

Stonehenge, in south-west England, was erected between *c.* 3000 and 1600 BC in three different stages and is the only stone circle in the world to have lintels. Standing at the end of an avenue 550 m long, the whole structure is orientated towards the sunrise of the summer (or possibly mid-winter) solstice. Its outer border is a bank and ditch 125 m in diameter, and the sanctuary itself consists of five concentric elements: an outer sarsen circle, an outer bluestone circle, inner sarsen trilithons, an inner bluestone horseshoe-shaped formation and an 'Altar Stone', a single slab of sandstone.

Stonehenge originally consisted of about 166 stones, although many have long since disappeared. The outer sarsen circle itself, 32 m in diameter, had thirty standing stones, joined together by heavy lintels. The stones were transported over long distances: the sarsens, weighing on average about 26 tonnes, came from the Marlborough Downs, 29 km away, but the bluestones were brought from the Preseli Hills in Wales, 217 km away, partly by sea, which implies a highly developed social organization as well as remarkable technological skill.

This monumental structure marks the emergence of circular geometry in Bronze Age architecture. As a 'solar observatory', Stonehenge would have served to fix the calendar, to establish the dates of festivals, and to provide the setting for religious rites in keeping with the 'megalithic civilization'. The latter extended from the Near East to the Mediterranean, and from Spain to northern Europe. Stonehenge captured the movements of the stars.

Left Stonehenge 'reconstructed' in the 18th century, when it was believed to have been a Druid temple.
Right One of the Stonehenge trilithons – two huge standing stones perfectly balanced with their lintel.
Opposite The megalithic circle in the landscape of Salisbury Plain, which stretches as far as the eye can see.
Fold-out The colossal blocks of Stonehenge, laid out to form an observatory.

GREAT MONUMENTS
OF THE ANCIENT WORLD

With 119 illustrations, 99 in colour

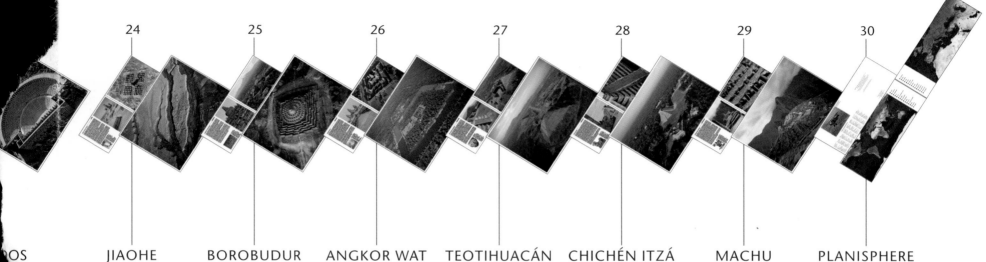

24   25   26   27   28   29   30

JIAOHE

A CITY IN THE FAR WEST OF CHINA

China
Asia

3rd century BC–
12th century AD

A natural fortress, this city is flanked by rocks up to 30 m high. It acted as a defence against invasion by nomadic peoples of Central Asia, then became a stopping place for caravans, and finally an important Buddhist centre: the traces of a city abandoned in the 12th century AD.

BOROBUDUR

THE GREAT STUPA TO THE GLORY OF THE BUDDHA

Indonesia
South-east Asia

8th–9th centuries AD

This cosmological representation has six square-shaped storeys (the earth) and three concentric circular levels (the heavens). The architecture of this imposing stupa was designed to be seen by the gods, from above. Bas-reliefs and statues depict scenes from the life of the Buddha.

ANGKOR WAT

THE GREAT KHMER TEMPLE

Cambodia
South-east Asia

12th–13th centuries AD

The temple at Angkor Wat covers a vast area of almost 200 hectares. Surrounded by a series of walls, it is the huge central square that dominates, with its quincunx of five mitre-shaped towers: a symbol of the wealth of the Khmer.

TEOTIHUACÁN

A PRE-COLUMBIAN CITY OF THE GODS

Mexico
Central America

c. 1st century BC–
6th century AD

This great city, on a high plateau, covers an area of 20 km² and is dominated by the pyramids of the Sun and the Moon, which are on a scale comparable to the pyramids of Giza. The city thrived until the 6th century AD, when it disappeared.

CHICHÉN ITZÁ

IN THE HEART OF THE MAYA WORLD

Mexico
Central America

10th–12th centuries AD

In Yucatán, this Maya city emerged from the forest, and with it the Castillo pyramid, which dominates the site, the Temple of the Warriors, the terrible feathered serpents protecting the sanctuary, and the chacmool, where the hearts of sacrificial victims were placed.

MACHU PICCHU

GUARDIAN OF THE RAINFOREST

Peru
South America

15–16th centuries AD

When it was discovered in 1911, this Inca city was virtually intact. The temples, the houses, the homes of the chiefs, the priests' sacrificial altars and the steep artificial terraces all reflected the city's centralized organization, hierarchical structures and collective economic system.

PLANISPHERE

A helicopter enables us to see whole sites and individual monuments from tens of metres above; with a satellite image, we can see areas from thousands of kilometres away. Aerial photography today benefits from a wide range of possibilities, showing us views that our ancestors could scarcely have imagined.

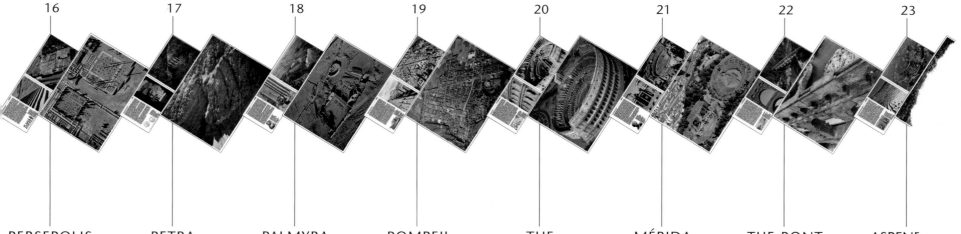

| 16 | 17 | 18 | 19 | 20 | 21 | 22 | 23 |

PERSEPOLIS
CAPITAL CITY OF THE GREAT KINGS OF PERSIA

Iran
Middle East

515–331 BC

Persepolis was built by the great kings of Persia, renowned enemies of the Greeks, who lived in splendour thanks to the tributes of their submissive people. With its palaces and halls covered in bas-reliefs, the city was beautiful, but Alexander the Great is said to have had it burned down in revenge for the Persian sack of Athens.

PETRA
CAPITAL OF TRADE WITH THE EAST

Jordan
Near East

4th century BC–
1st century AD

This was a camel-drivers' capital that became rich through its east–west trade. Monuments were carved into the red sandstone, boasting tall façades decorated with columns and capitals, cylindrical tholoi and pediments, and banqueting halls and funerary loculi were built in the rock itself.

PALMYRA
CARAVAN CITY OF THE DESERT

Syria
Near East

AD 32–272

The oasis of Palmyra, in the heart of the Syrian desert, is where East meets West. The city's inter-tribal temple, dedicated to three local deities, and its grand avenues, lined with hundreds of sumptuous columns, bear testament to its former splendour.

POMPEII
A CITY UNDER THE ASHES

Italy
Europe

1st century AD

One of the most remarkable insights into the past has emerged from a natural catastrophe, the eruption of Mount Vesuvius on 24 August, AD 79: the streets of Pompeii are a history lesson, and the city's houses seem suspended in time, awaiting the return of their inhabitants.

THE COLOSSEUM IN ROME
'BREAD AND CIRCUSES'

Italy
Europe

1st century AD

The Emperor Vespasian gave the citizens of Rome the greatest games arena of all time: an amphitheatre of impressive dimensions (188 m in diameter and 50 m high), designed to hold fights between wild beasts, gladiatorial combats and nautical shows.

MÉRIDA
A ROMAN CITY IN SPAIN

Spain
Europe

25 BC–2nd century AD

At the far west of the Roman Empire, Mérida was the capital of the province of Lusitania: its theatre, with sumptuous colonnaded porticos, and its amphitheatre, which had a seating capacity of 14,000, bear testament to the city's former prestige.

THE PONT DU GARD
AN AQUEDUCT FOR NÎMES

France
Europe

19 BC

Baths, pools, springs: as far as water was concerned, Roman citizens did not go without. The Romans had to learn to overcome obstacles and devise innovative constructions in order to channel this precious resource. The Pont du Gard is their masterpiece.

ASPEND
THE BEST-PRESE ROMAN THEA

Turkey
Near East

2nd century AD

With its forty rows of seats and capac of 13,000 spectato this theatre provide the stage for a whole host of different performances: tragedy, mime, dance, singing, and fantastic or satirical interludes. From West to East, Rome exported the symbols of its urbanization and culture.

THE STONE TEMPLE OF MNAJDRA

The first major examples of Western monumental architecture are to be found on the tiny islets of the Maltese archipelago in the heart of the Mediterranean. The colossal edifices have stood there for over 5,000 years. These megalithic temples, excavated in the early 19th century, comprise units of several oval chambers lined with mighty orthostats (standing blocks), which were originally covered with corbelled vaults and linked together by large doors.

As well as Mnajdra, which is one of the best preserved of all these sanctuaries, the temples of Hagar Qim, Tarxien (which lay buried under farmland in Valletta until its discovery), the underground chambers of the Hal Saflieni hypogeum (which contained the remains of thousands of bodies), and the temple at Ggantija, on the island of Gozo, all bear witness to the dynamism of a culture that thrived from *c.* 4000 to 2500 BC, prior to the Bronze Age. This architecture is therefore even older than the great pyramids of Egypt.

The buildings have been found to hold a host of stone furnishings: altars, walls fitted out as sacristies, apparently to receive offerings, and hidden holies of holies, which may have once been used by the oracles of the cults that were practised there. Many of the objects found – statues of goddesses, spiral decorations, animal reliefs – lead us to imagine a religion that was dominated by a mother goddess, whose influence subsequently spread throughout megalithic Europe.

Left One of the statues of the 'Great Goddess', found on many sites in Malta.
Right A doorway in the megalithic temple of Mnajdra, on the cliffs overlooking the Mediterranean.
Opposite The main sanctuary of the temple, 5,200 years old, consisting of two oval rooms lined with massive vertical blocks.
Fold-out The temple of Mnajdra, out in the arid landscape of southern Malta.

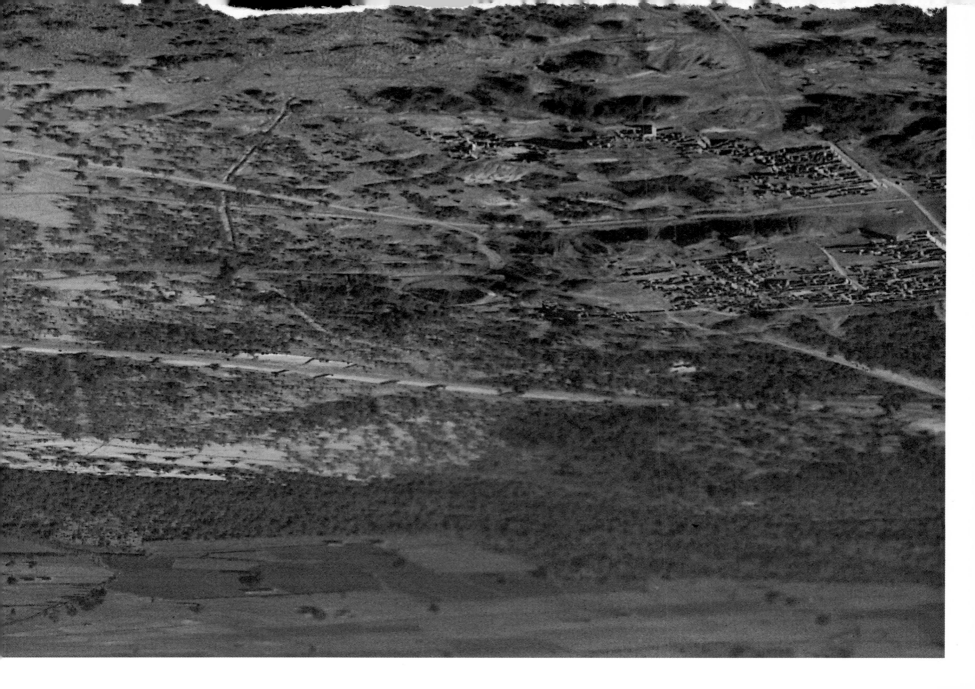

CITY ON THE BANKS OF THE INDUS

The emergence of huge cities such as Mohenjo-daro and Harappa in the Indus valley can be compared to that of the first Mesopotamian cities in south-west Asia. Harappa was first recognized as an archaeological site in 1826 but it was damaged by looters in the mid-19th century. Mohenjo-daro was rediscovered in the early 20th century, but it was not until the 1920s – when excavations were conducted at both Harappa and Mohenjo-daro – that its true significance was realized.

Mohenjo-daro shows evidence of a highly sophisticated social structure – with its grid-pattern layout (streets branching off at right angles), an advanced hydraulic system with conveyance and drainage of water, private and public baths (based on vast reserves that could cope with seasonal variations), and standard forms of brick – together with a powerful hierarchy and central government. It also had trade relations with towns on the Euphrates as well as with Persia and Afghanistan.

Nevertheless, this urban world on the Indus was predominantly agricultural, and the people lived mainly on wheat and cattle. Their storage techniques were just as advanced as those of their transport, and broad streets and ramps allowed access for carts. Art, of which there are some fine but comparatively rare specimens, and religion (no temples have yet come to light), do not seem to have been regarded as essential in a society whose main preoccupation was the fulfilment of daily needs. Ceramics and statues, including a hieratic priest-king with elongated eyes and a beard, some seals decorated with animals, and signs in an untranslatable language are the only items that remain of a people that lived between *c.* 2500 and 2000 BC and then mysteriously disappeared.

Left A small-scale terracotta model of a cart.
Right On either side of the arrow-straight, paved streets are houses made of baked, well-aligned bricks.
Opposite The citadel of Mohenjo-daro, with its courtyards and passages going off at right angles.
Fold-out The complete site, in the alluvial plain of the Indus, with its two centres – the lower town (left) and the citadel (right) on a mound some 15 m high.

THE SUMERIAN CAPITAL OF MESOPOTAMIA

Excavations have shown that the city of Ur, on the Euphrates, was occupied from at least 4000 BC. The Bible names it as Abraham's homeland, situated in ancient Chaldea, now part of Iraq. This capital of the Sumerians owed its importance to the cult of the Moon God (Nanna or Sin). Its civilization and script date back to the First Dynasty (*c.* 2563–*c.* 2387 BC), and at that time it was an important cultural centre in Mesopotamia. In the 1930s the great archaeologist Sir Leonard Woolley discovered some impressive royal tombs there, which housed various treasures of gold and silver: vases, weapons, jewelry, a harp with a bull decoration – all buried along with the sacrificial victims who accompanied the deceased in death.

The Third Dynasty of Ur (*c.* 2112–*c.* 2004 BC) saw further development of the city and its architecture. The pinnacle of this magnificence was the ziggurat, the Mesopotamian 'pyramid', which has been used as a model for images of the Tower of Babel. Flights of steps lead to the summit of this artificial mountain, which houses the sanctuary and the sacrificial altar. From the top of the ziggurat, whose corners are orientated according to the points of the compass, the astronomer-priests would observe the stars rising on the horizon. Surrounded by a wall, the temenos, the monumental ziggurat is 62 m by 43 m, 22 m high, incorporates some 40,000 m³ of materials, and dominates the nearby temples, the palace and the residential areas. This architecture of mudbricks faced with baked brick is laid out in a pattern of right angles. By contrast, the city itself is contained within an elliptical wall. To the north-west, there were quays lining the port on the Euphrates.

Left A tablet with cuneiform script – the earliest known writing system in the world.
Right A large axial flight of steps leading to the second level of the ziggurat.
Opposite The centre of Ur with the ziggurat (left), the palaces (centre) and the residential districts (right).
Fold-out The sloping walls and three ramps that buttress the massive structure of the ziggurat.

THE BEGINNINGS OF SYRIA

At the crossroads between the Mediterranean, Anatolia, Phoenicia and Mesopotamia, the Syrian plain was an intersecting point for a variety of influences, and the ancient city of Ebla (Tell Mardikh) benefited from all of these. From 2350 BC it was in contact with Sumer and Akkad, the cradles of Mesopotamian civilization, from which it inherited cuneiform writing and religious traditions. It enjoyed considerable influence of its own, because after it had been subject to the Third Dynasty of Ur, it governed a substantial empire in the Near East. This stretched from Mari, a powerful city in the east of Syria, to the very limits of the Mesopotamian world. It was captured by the Akkadian King Naram-Sin in c. 2250 BC, and finally disappeared in the 15th century BC, when it is mentioned for the last time: an inscription dating from the reign of the pharaoh Thutmose III, in c. 1450 BC, describes Ebla as a stopping-place for Egyptian troops on their way to the Euphrates.

In 1975 some 15,000 tablets of cuneiform writing were discovered, comprising religious, legal, diplomatic and commercial texts that offered a great deal of insight into the way the city developed. They contain evidence of local warfare, for example, and reveal that the king of Ebla had 80,000 sheep in his possession. Excavations also brought to light a large number of exceptional objects, which bear witness to an advanced culture that spread throughout this region during the second millennium BC. Ebla contained a royal palace in the centre with an archive building, a large temple dedicated to the goddess Ishtar, and various sanctuaries in the lower town, as well as a monumental gate in the south-western wall.

Left Seal impression from the royal palace at Ebla.
Right Excavations of the plain south of Aleppo began in 1964 to uncover the remains of the city.
Opposite An aerial view reveals stores and residences with courtyards.
Fold-out The city of Ebla covers an area of 95 hectares, surrounded by an irregular earthwork wall.

THE TOMBS OF THE PHARAOHS

Close to Memphis – the capital of Egypt when it was united in the third millennium BC – the pharaohs of the Old Kingdom, Khufu (Cheops), Khafre (Chephren) and Menkaure (Mycerinus), erected their eternal homes on the desert plateau bordering the fertile Nile Valley. The colossal size marks the climax of a fashion that began with the brick mastabas (simple rectangular burial chambers) at Abydos, and progressed through Djoser's step pyramid at Saqqara to the first major pyramids at Meidum and Dahshur.

The pyramid of Khufu, built in *c.* 2551–*c.* 2528 BC, is the largest of the three pyramids at Giza. In order to construct it, first it was necessary to level the rocky terrain and to mark out the square base with each side (230 m long) facing the cardinal points. The four sides, which slope at an angle of 52 degrees and were originally faced with polished limestone, all present the perfect symmetry of the triangular form. The pyramid rises to a height of 146 m, and comprises 2,650,000 m³ of local limestone, as well as blocks of granite transported over 935 km by raft from Aswan, each weighing about 2.5 tonnes and used for load-bearing. In total, the materials used weighed about 6,800,000 tonnes. Within this mighty structure, the actual burial chamber measures no more than 5.23 m by 10.47 m.

The construction of this colossal edifice is believed to have taken about twenty-three years. In addition to the burial chamber, it has a valley temple, a mortuary temple, a covered causeway, a surrounding wall, and pits for the funeral boats. Egyptians of the Old Kingdom had no knowledge of the wheel, lifting 'machines', or beasts of burden, and the pyramid was built solely by labourers – an indication of the whole nation's collective faith in the afterlife.

Left Soldiers and scholars from the Egyptian expedition on top of the pyramid of Khufu.
Right The pyramid of Khufu. On the first level, the blocks that form the base are 1.5 m high.
Opposite The complete site, with mastabas crowded all round the pyramids of Khufu (left), Khafre (centre) and Menkaure (right).
Fold-out The top of the pyramid of Khafre, still with its limestone facing.

THE TEMPLE OF QUEEN HATSHEPSUT

In New Kingdom Egypt, the capital city was Thebes, situated in Upper Egypt. The year 1473 BC saw the beginning of a dark drama of jealousy between Queen Hatshepsut and her nephew (and stepson) Thutmose III, whom she succeeded in keeping under guard and away from power for fifteen years. Having made herself pharaoh and assumed the crown of Upper and Lower Egypt, Hatshepsut reigned until 1458 BC, along with her chief steward, the architect Senenmut. He was the one who designed a mortuary temple for her, with terraces built into the cliffs of Deir el-Bahri, at the foot of the great rock faces, behind which lie the Valley of the Kings, where the pharaohs were buried.

Senenmut was inspired by an example from the Middle Kingdom, built half a millennium earlier: the temple of the pharaoh Montuhotep II (r. c. 2010–c. 1960 BC). Both of these neighbouring shrines have ascending ramps that link the terraces to the finely decorated porticos. Both also dig deep into the rock, where a vaulted chamber carved into the stone provided the setting for rituals associated with the cult of the dead monarch. The bas-relief decorations of Hatshepsut's temple, illustrating her expedition to Punt (south of the Red Sea) and her many other exploits, form painted galleries in the shade of the porticos. In front of the third and final portico stand pillars in the image of the deified queen, wearing the false beard of the pharaohs.

Since 1962 archaeological excavations have shown that Thutmose III, once he had assumed power, built his own mortuary temple between those of Montuhotep II and the queen. It was destroyed by a catastrophic rockfall, which crushed the porticos and the entrance ramps, and remained forgotten for 3,000 years.

Left Bas-reliefs at Deir el-Bahri of Hatshepsut's divine birth.
Right Hatshepsut represented as pharaoh in front of the third portico.
Opposite The three levels of colonnades that seem to emerge from the rock.
Fold-out The full scale of the temple, with its terraces linked by sloping ramps. To the left is the temple of Montuhotep II.

THE GREAT TEMPLE OF AMUN: A CITY OF PRIESTS

In Thebes, which was the new capital of ancient Egypt when it was at the height of its powers, the great Temple of Karnak, whose construction was directed by the priests of Amun, became virtually a city within a city, wielding an authority that rivalled that of the pharaoh himself.

The construction of the Temple of Amun began during the Middle Kingdom. Around 2000 BC a simple granite sanctuary was built that has now disappeared. To this were added six pylons (monumental entrances flanked by two towers), an increasing number of courtyards, encircling walls and hypostyle halls (in which the ceiling rests on a number of columns). The temple is really a collection of buildings erected during the 18th and 19th dynasties, between c. 1580 and 1200 BC, and completed in c. 300 BC. The finished temple of Amun was 380 m long and 100 m across, and it was surrounded by a brick wall 600 m by 750 m. The Temple of Amun was then joined by the Temples of Ptah and Khonsu, as well as those of the goddess Mut and god Montu, enclosed within their own walls.

Mainly the work of Seti I and Ramesses II (c. 1290–c. 1213 BC), the hypostyle hall of the Temple of Amun, built on the back of the second pylon, covers an area of 100 m by 55 m. Its one hundred and thirty-four columns rise to a height of 20 m. Its central aisle, constructed by Amenhotep III after 1360 BC, rests on twelve even taller pillars (23 m), whose solid capitals have a circumference of 15 m. The walls and columns are covered with bas-reliefs, which still bear traces of paint and depict scenes from the cult and great deeds of the pharaoh.

Left The god Amun (centre) facing the pharaoh.

Right The enormous columns in the hypostyle hall.

Opposite Aerial view of the hall, showing the layout of the columns and lintels, and the central aisle (left).

Fold-out Overall view of the Temple of Amun: the first pylon, the great court with the Temple of Ramesses III (c. 1187–c. 1156 BC) on the right, the second pylon (ruined), the hypostyle hall and, beyond that, more courts, pylons and halls.

THE 'TEMPLE OF A MILLION YEARS'

Dating from the 19th dynasty, the mortuary temple that the mighty pharaoh Ramesses II constructed in *c.* 1250 BC at Thebes, on the 'banks of the dead' at the foot of Sheikh Abd el-Qurnah, is in a relatively poor state of repair. Nevertheless, it is typical of the great monuments that the rulers of Egypt built in order to perpetuate their own cults, along with their tombs on the other side of the hill, in the narrow, arid Valley of the Kings. Behind a pylon (half-ruined) is a courtyard surrounded by porticos, leading to a hypostyle hall. Everywhere there are bas-reliefs that depict battle scenes, commemorating the great pharaoh's victories.

By contrast, the outbuildings – stores, warehouses, depositories for offerings, workshops and administrative buildings – have withstood the ravages of time. They are covered with mud-bricks, and have parallel vaults consisting of oblique crossed arches that buttress one another. This shows that the Egyptians had completely mastered the technique of the arch, even though they scarcely ever made this architectural feature from stone.

The mortuary temples of the New Kingdom stand on the edges of an area that is irrigated by the Nile and is criss-crossed by canals; boats coming from Thebes could dock opposite the entrance on ceremonial days, bringing priests to honour the dead ruler and perform the rites of immortality. The king, whose mummy lay in the tomb that had been dug into the hill, maintained close links with the priests who were charged for eternity with his cult, for his afterlife depended on the loyalty of the temple servants.

Left The temple as seen by a traveller in the 19th century.
Right Pillars with an effigy of the pharaoh Ramesses II as the god Osiris, symbolizing resurrection. A gigantic head of the king lies in the foreground.
Opposite The hypostyle hall of the Ramesseum, surrounded by storerooms.
Fold-out Sheikh Abd el-Qurnah (at the foot of the hill) and, on the edge of the fertile plain, the temple surrounded by a brick wall.

THE PYRAMIDS OF SUDAN

The vast region that stretches over 800 km up the Nile from Aswan, heading towards Upper Nubia (modern-day Sudan) as far as the fourth cataract, was well known from the time of the Old Kingdom. During the 15th century BC, Thutmose III built temples at Gebel Barkal. In the 7th century BC the kingdom of Meroë, which initially repulsed the Egyptians in the north, succeeded in conquering the whole of Egypt. Following the model of the small pyramids the Nubians had seen at Qurnah, the Meroite kings constructed a significant number of steeply angled pyramids (70 degrees) at Meroë, though never exceeding 20–24 m in height. The remains of the Nubian kings are buried there, surrounded by treasures that proved a temptation to 19th-century looters and archaeologists.

The thirty monuments in the cemetery north of Meroë are arranged in a unique manner: adjoining the pyramid is a sanctuary preceded by a pylon, and there are one or two subterranean burial chambers accessible by way of a fairly steep slope. These pyramids, built between 270 BC and AD 350, contained gold ornaments that were at first believed to be fake but then, through the work of the German archaeologist Richard Lepsius, were found to be authentic. Although these structures do not have the size, grandeur or masses of materials found in the great pyramids of Giza, they bear witness to the influence exerted by Egyptian civilization.

Left The pyramid of Queen Amanishakheto at Meroë.
Right The sovereigns of Meroë built small, steep-sided pyramids.
Opposite The pyramids, which were built over underground burial chambers, were often sacked by treasure-hunters.
Fold-out The northern necropolis at Meroë contains several pyramids erected in the desert, with a chapel in front of them and an entrance pylon.

THE FEUDAL AGE IN GREECE

The Mycenaeans were the dominant force in Greece after 1600 BC, and their buildings – especially the city of Mycenae – were fortresses. The military and palatial architecture of the Mycenaeans, which reached its zenith in the 13th century BC, is all about power, with walls made of huge stone blocks and gates that reinforced the formidable strength of these bastions. The enormous lintel that dominates the entrance to the city is guarded by two lions – with their front paws on an altar – separated by a column. As for the palaces of the warlords, they are the crowning glory of the city, with their reception area, or megaron, installed behind a court-yard and porch. An antechamber precedes the throne room, which is flanked by apartments. Within this Homeric setting, it is easy to picture the return of Odysseus and the massacre of the suitors.

In the Lower City, the circle of royal graves where the Mycenaeans buried their rulers forms a huge circular structure, ringed by standing stones. The treasures from the 16th century BC, discovered in 1876 by renowned archaeologist Heinrich Schliemann, were buried there: gold funerary masks, sumptuous gold and silver work, and weapons decorated with hunting scenes in gold and silver. More tombs were erected later outside the city with domes (the Treasury of Atreus and the Treasury of Clytemnestra), but they had already been looted by the time they were discovered.

Left The gold 'mask of Agamemnon', found in grave 5 of the circle of royal burials.
Right The monumental gate of Mycenae, its tympanum (the triangular block above the lintel) decorated with lions guarding the entrance.
Opposite Inside the wall surrounding Mycenae, the circle of tombs that contained the royal sepulchres and their rich treasures.
Fold-out Between two ravines, the city of Mycenae: a labyrinth of houses line the slope leading to the palace, which stands at the top.

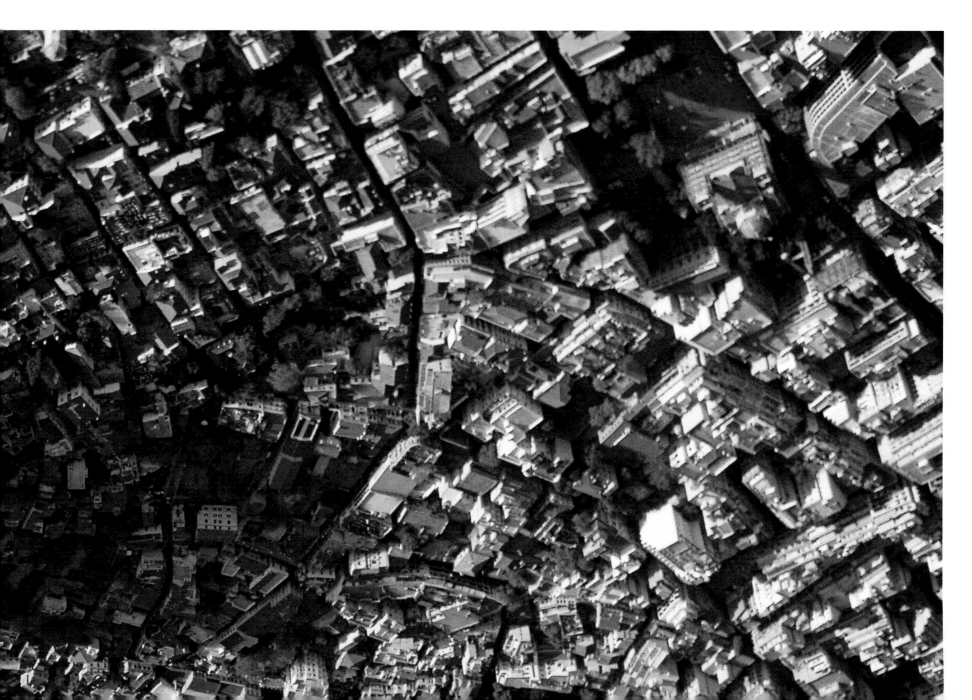

'THE CITY OF THE GODS'

On the site of an ancient fortress surrounded by steep rocks, where once the Athenians used to take refuge, they built the Acropolis – a raised citadel dedicated to the gods of the city and, in particular, to the goddess Athena from whom it takes its name.

On this hill was built the most famous of all Greek temples, the Parthenon, dedicated to Athena Parthenos ('Virgin') – the work of Pheidias (sculptor of statues) and Iktinos (architect, with Kallikrates), begun in 447 BC. A veritable symphony of rhythms and proportions, the Parthenon is the crown of the Acropolis, and its classical authority sets the tone for all Greek art. The ground plan – eight Doric columns at the ends and seventeen at the sides (a total of forty-six columns) – as well as the materials used (Paros marble) and, above all, the quality of its sculptures have made it one of the greatest masterpieces of all time.

The layout of the other buildings on the Acropolis are also vivid testimony to the urban skills of the Greeks: the Propylaia – the colonnaded entrance to the site – recalls the military past and welcomes processions during festivals such as the 'Panathenaia'. Two other temples, the Erechtheion and the Temple of Athena Nike ('Victory'), stand along the sacred route open to the citizens of Athens.

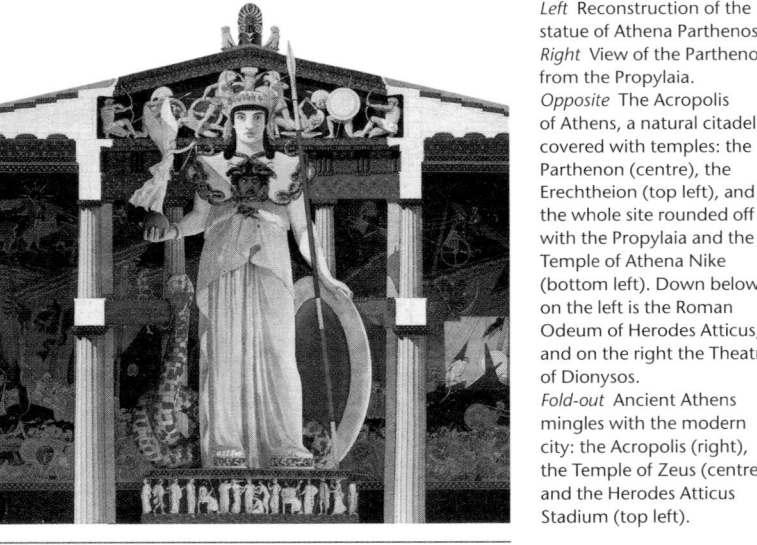

Left Reconstruction of the statue of Athena Parthenos.
Right View of the Parthenon from the Propylaia.
Opposite The Acropolis of Athens, a natural citadel covered with temples: the Parthenon (centre), the Erechtheion (top left), and the whole site rounded off with the Propylaia and the Temple of Athena Nike (bottom left). Down below on the left is the Roman Odeum of Herodes Atticus, and on the right the Theatre of Dionysos.
Fold-out Ancient Athens mingles with the modern city: the Acropolis (right), the Temple of Zeus (centre) and the Herodes Atticus Stadium (top left).

THE ISLAND OF APOLLO IN THE HEART OF THE AEGEAN

From 478 BC the island of Delos – the legendary birthplace of Apollo, who was worshipped by the Ionians – became the centre of the Athenian League, which brought together a group of Greek cities united against the Persians. The treasure that had been kept in the Temple of Apollo was subsequently transferred to Athens. Delos, situated in the Cyclades and nestling in the shelter of the island of Mykonos, was partly protected from the gusts of the meltemi wind.

The island was soon covered with temples, and its port was declared sacred. As well as those sanctuaries dedicated to Apollo, temples were built for Leto, Apollo's mother, which together form the Letoon near the Terrace of the Lions – ancient sculptures from the 7th century BC. Within this narrow space are crowds of secular buildings: the agoras (public squares), the palaestra (sports ground), buildings used for religious or political events, and grand private residences with porticoed courtyards paved with remarkable mosaics, many of which survive.

This tiny area became the heart of the Cyclades. Its size did not prevent it from being the economic centre of ancient Greece, the crossroads for international trade, and a veritable stock exchange capable of dealing in all the currencies – drachmas, staters, tetradrachmas – that were circulating in the Mediterranean basin at the time. With all this wealth, Delos was frequently sacked, but it later became a free port under the Romans, and prospered once again.

Left Reconstruction of an Ionian house.
Right The so-called House of Hermes (2nd century BC), built around a two-storey atrium with a well, fed by a cistern.
Opposite Partial view of the island of Delos, with its oval lake (now dried up) bordered by the Agora of the Italians (2nd century BC). It shows the complex of the ruined Temple of Apollo (centre) and the theatre area (top).
Fold-out Close-up of the theatre area with its rich houses and their atria and mosaic parterres.

TEMPLES OF MAGNA GRAECIA

The Greeks founded many colonies in southern Italy (Taranto, Kroton, Sybaris) and in Sicily (Agrigento, Selinunte, Segesta), and in the town of Paestum – originally Poseidonia – south of Naples, there are three Doric temples that have remained almost intact. All three are orientated in the same direction (east–west), but they are staggered in terms of time: the Sanctuary of Hera I (popularly misnamed the 'Basilica') dates from c. 550–525 BC; the Temple of Athena (formerly known as the Temple of Ceres) – at the other end of the site – was built in c. 500 BC; and the most recent (the Temple of Hera II, formerly thought to be the Temple of Poseidon) originates from c. 460 BC, which makes it roughly contemporary with the Parthenon. Thus they trace an evolution from ancient to classical architecture.

A harbour town, Paestum was founded in the 7th century BC by colonists from Sybaris. It is surrounded by walls punctuated with towers. Its wealth was based on trade and the fertile plains around it, irrigated by the river Sele – a prosperity that was prolonged by some judicious political decisions and an unshakeable loyalty to Rome during the time of the Republic. However, it fell victim to numerous invasions, and the barbarians ravaged the country and broke the aqueducts. These continued to discharge their water and flooded the countryside, transforming it into a swamp. The last inhabitants were driven away by the onset of disease, and the abandoned temples soon disappeared beneath the vegetation. It was not until the Bourbon King Charles (1716–88), later Charles III of Spain, was seeking a coastal route that these ancient monuments were rediscovered. Paestum's importance was recognized and it became one of the most famous ancient sites.

Left A drawing of the temples when they were rediscovered.
Right The ancient columns and Doric capitals of the Temple of Hera I (left) and the façade of the classical Temple of Hera II, with its frieze of triglyphs supporting the pediment (right).
Opposite The Temple of Athena.
Fold-out View of part of Paestum, showing the symmetrical layout of the two temples of Hera.

THE ORACLE OF APOLLO IN GREEK ASIA MINOR

The Temple of Didyma, near Miletus, was dedicated to Apollo and was one of those great centres – like Delphi – to which people came in order to consult an oracle. Priests would receive those who came for advice concerning different areas of private or public life, and they acted as intermediaries with the prophetess who, from within the sanctuary, would invoke Apollo and ask him the relevant questions.

Like other Greek temples in Asia (the Temple of Artemis at Ephesus, and the great Temple of Samos), Didyma is a huge building over 100 m long, Ionic in style, with a cella (the inner area of an ancient temple) surrounded by two rows of columns comprising one hundred and twenty-two shafts, 20 m high. The first temple of Didyma, to which Croesus – king of neighbouring Lydia – had contributed, was destroyed by the Persians during the Persian Wars that followed the revolt of the Ionian cities. In 332 BC Alexander the Great decided to rebuild it, but the work went on for over four hundred and fifty years, into the reigns of the Roman emperors Trajan and Hadrian (2nd century AD).

The Temple of Didyma is outstanding for the opulence of its Hellenistic decoration. Carved in marble, it is full of remarkably detailed reliefs: the sculpted decorations at the base of the columns combine confident draughtsmanship with extraordinary elegance. The Ionic volutes of the capitals, the Medusa faces and the griffins on the friezes are all virtuoso works of art. Didyma is thus a mixture of large-scale architecture and meticulously executed detail. After being transformed into a church, this colossal structure was shattered by an earthquake in 1493.

Left Decorative design and frieze with griffins.
Right Grand interior staircase descending to the open-air court (*adyton*) and leading to the *naiskos* (a small temple) that housed the oracle.
Opposite and fold-out The temple on its podium ringed with terraces. After offering up a sacrifice on the circular altar, those seeking advice would wait for the oracle's response in the pronaos (a vestibule just in front of the interior court).

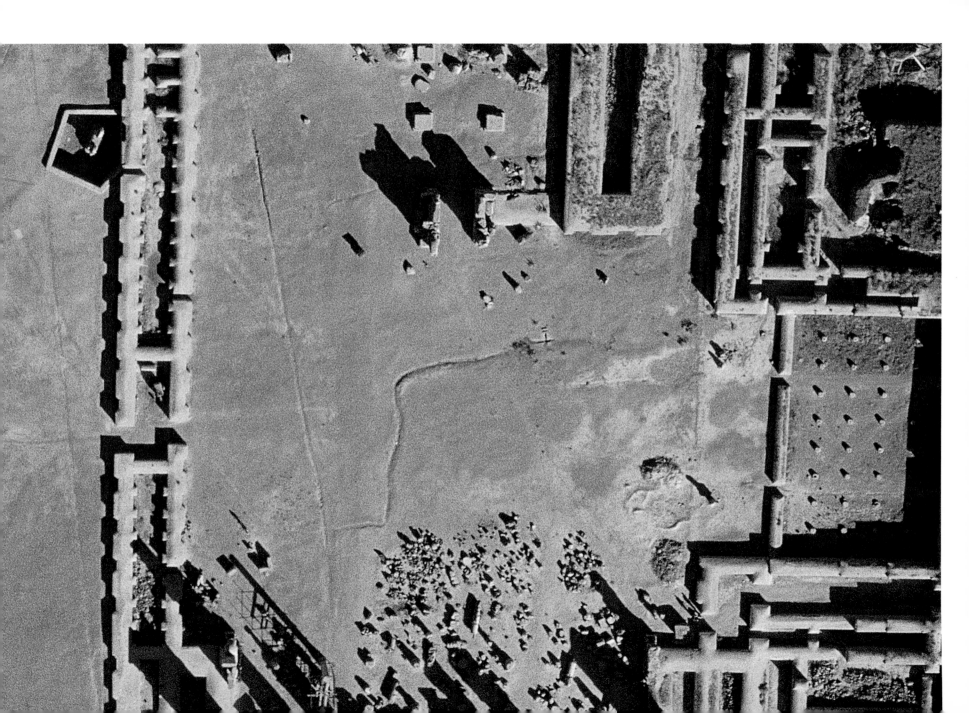

CAPITAL CITY OF THE GREAT KINGS OF PERSIA

In the heart of Fars, the Persian land which the conquests of Cyrus II (*c.* 585–*c.* 529 BC) and Cambyses II (529–522 BC) took to the head of a vast empire, Persepolis was the centre for the court rituals of the Achaemenid dynasty. Founded by Darius the Great in *c.* 515 BC, and completed by his son Xerxes I and grandson Artaxerxes I, this royal city was constructed on an artificial terrace 500 m by 300 m. The buildings were designed to celebrate the Iranian New Year ('Norouz'), and greeted the representatives of subject nations, from Egypt to Afghanistan and India, and from Central Asia to Mesopotamia and Arabia, including Anatolia and Greek Asia Minor. It was to Persepolis that the tribute bearers came to pay homage to the great king, as can be seen from the procession that fills the bas-reliefs at the base of the Apadana, the ceremonial hall built by Darius.

The palaces followed an orthogonal plan and all had colonnades supporting wooden roofs (hypostyle halls). The Apadana was the most accomplished of these: preceded by galleries with double porticos, the hall (60.5 m²) was covered by a cedar roof, which was held up by thirty-six columns, each 20 m high, with capitals shaped like the heads of bulls, griffins and lions. The columns had the same proportions as those in the Ionic temples at Ephesus and Samos, for it was Ionian architects and sculptors (from Greek Asia Minor) who built this masterpiece, as the founding decree indicates. In this sumptuous palace, the Persian and Median dignitaries would come in solemn procession to make their sacrifices and hold their ritual feasts in the presence of the king, who would preside over the ceremony. Alexander the Great, when he conquered Persepolis in 331 BC, is said to have had it burned down in revenge for the Persian sack of Athens.

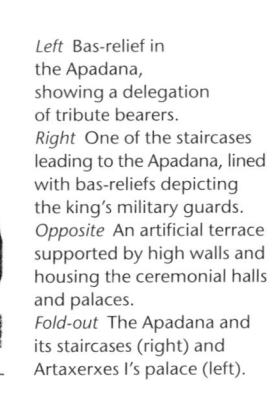

Left Bas-relief in the Apadana, showing a delegation of tribute bearers.
Right One of the staircases leading to the Apadana, lined with bas-reliefs depicting the king's military guards.
Opposite An artificial terrace supported by high walls and housing the ceremonial halls and palaces.
Fold-out The Apadana and its staircases (right) and Artaxerxes I's palace (left).

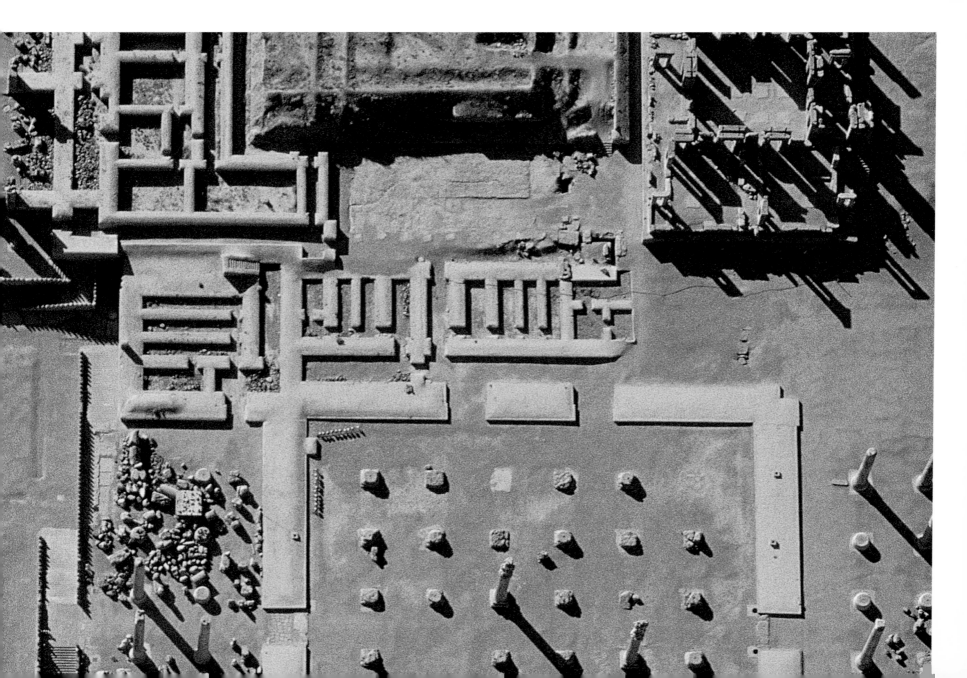

CAPITAL OF TRADE WITH THE EAST

At the heart of the sandstone massif of ancient Nabataea, between the ports of Aqaba and Gaza, Petra was the centre of east–west trade during the Greco-Roman era. Its kings made this impregnable city between the Mediterranean and the Red Sea into a trading centre that dealt in all the most precious commodities. Thanks to the wealth procured through incense and other such luxury goods – exchanged for *objets d'art*, bronze statuettes, glassware and wine – the Arab traders grew rich. In Petra they employed Greek architects and Alexandrian sculptors to embellish their camel-drivers' capital.

The monuments are carved in red sandstone. Between the 4th century BC and the 1st century AD, armies of sculptors came to carve tall façades decorated with columns and Corinthian capitals, cylindrical tholoi (dome-shaped tombs) and pediments with urns. In the rock itself they built banqueting halls and funerary loculi. It was there that they performed the rites that turned kings into gods, and held ceremonies and sumptuous feasts in the presence of twelve guests and the king himself. One Greek traveller reported: 'There are thirteen in number, together with two musicians, at the feast.'

One prosperous reign succeeded another. It was during the long reign of Aretas IV (9 BC–AD 40) that the Treasury of the Pharaoh and its grandiose classical façade are believed to have been constructed. Malchos II and Rabel II, between AD 40 and 106, were the last Nabataean sovereigns, giving way to the troops of the Roman Emperor Trajan. It was not until the beginning of the 19th century that the Swiss explorer Johann Ludwig Burckhardt finally rescued the glories of Petra from oblivion.

Left Coins from Petra.
Right Carved into the sandstone, the façade of the Treasury of the Pharaoh, with its pediments and central tholos.
Opposite Al-Dayr, another building carved into the rock on the outskirts of the site, and long forgotten until it was rediscovered through aerial photography.
Fold-out On the edge of the city stands a line of tombs at the foot of a huge rock face.

CARAVAN CITY OF THE DESERT

The fortunes of Palmyra rose as those of Petra began to wane. From then on, trade with the East passed through the Persian Gulf and Mesopotamia: the caravan route crossed the Euphrates and reached the Mediterranean ports via the oasis of Palmyra. Here, between Babylon and Damascus, the Arab–Aramaean sovereigns created a centre for import and export that rapidly developed into a flourishing market.

Palmyra's strategic position attracted the Romans. The Emperor Tiberius supported the construction of an inter-tribal temple, bringing together three local deities, Bel, Aglibol and Yarhibol, whose effigies are dressed in Roman armour. In the south-east of the city, in a huge square temenos and surrounded by porticos, is a temple built by architects and sculptors who came from Baalbek or Antioch; the sanctuary, or cella, was inaugurated in AD 32. The Temple of Bel combines Greco-Roman elements with local and Mesopotamian features, a mixture of influences that gives it a classical and at the same time oriental appearance. The city's grand avenues bore testament to its splendour. They were lined with hundreds of columns, each of which honoured a donor, whose effigy was prominently displayed in bronze on a console. This 'genealogy of the city's fortunes' was completed by the statues of Palmyrans, stretched out on funeral beds in their tombs, and by busts closing the loculi in the towers of the dead.

During a critical period for the Roman Empire, in the 3rd century AD, Queen Zenobia dreamed of making Palmyra the capital of a kingdom encompassing Egypt and Syria. In AD 272 Aurelian put a stop to this by capturing the rebel queen, thus safeguarding the power of the Empire.

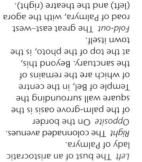
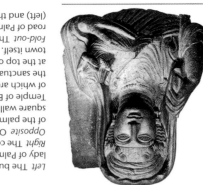

Left The bust of an aristocratic lady of Palmyra.

Right The colonnaded avenues.

Opposite On the border of the palm-grove oasis is the square wall surrounding the Temple of Bel, in the centre of which are the remains of the sanctuary. Beyond this, at the top of the photo, is the town itself.

Fold-out The great east–west road of Palmyra, with the agora (left) and the theatre (right).

A CITY UNDER THE ASHES

'Broad flames shone out in several places from Mount Vesuvius, which the darkness of the night contributed to render still brighter and clearer.... The sea seemed to roll back upon itself, and to be driven from its banks by the convulsive motion of the earth.... On the other side, a black and dreadful cloud, broken with rapid, zigzag flashes, revealed behind it variously shaped masses of flame: these last were like sheet-lightning, but much larger.... Soon afterwards, the cloud began to descend, and cover the sea.... The ashes now began to fall upon us.... I looked back; a dense dark mist seemed to be following us, spreading itself over the country like a cloud.... At last this dreadful darkness was dissipated by degrees, like a cloud or smoke; the real day returned, and even the sun shone out, though with a lurid light, like when an eclipse is coming on. Every object that presented itself to our eyes...seemed changed, being covered deep with ashes as if with snow.' This was the tragic night of 24 August, AD 79, when catastrophe struck the cities below Vesuvius, described here by Pliny the Younger.

To archaeologists, the buried city of Pompeii revealed not only statues, frescoes and scattered treasures, but also a symmetrically planned layout, with streets at right angles to one another and monumental buildings harmoniously integrated into the whole: the forum, centre of public life, temples on high podia, shops, places of entertainment. Along the paved streets were the dwellings – rich villas, family houses, laid out round enclosed gardens and porticos. Pompeii was a city for holiday-making, built under the influence of the Greeks, and very different from the insulae, or tenements, in the overcrowded residential districts of Rome or Ostia. In Pompeii, wealthy Romans could enjoy the pleasures of the good life.

Left The body of an inhabitant of Pompeii, in the same position in which he died. *Right* A paved street, lined with shops. Vesuvius can be seen in the background. *Opposite* One of the residential quarters of the city. *Fold-out* View of the site, showing the forum and its temples (left) and the theatre and the odeum (right).

'BREAD AND CIRCUSES'

The enormous arena of the Flavian Amphitheatre, known as the Colosseum and built to provide spectacular events for the public, is the biggest building in the imperial capital. It owes the name 'Colosseum' to the fact that it stands on the site of Nero's Colossus (a giant statue of the Emperor). It was commissioned by the Emperor Vespasian (r. AD 69–79) and inaugurated in the year AD 80 by his son Titus. The occasion was marked by three months of games, during which 2,000 gladiators and 9,000 wild animals were killed.

The building itself is elliptical in form, with a diameter of 188 m and a transverse axis of 156 m. It rises to a maximum height of 50 m through three storeys of arcades and a blind upper floor. Each storey contains eighty arches and is decorated in a different style: the first is Doric, the second Ionic, and the third Corinthian. The interior is an immense cavea (seating area), with regular terraces all round, capable of seating 70,000 spectators – approximately half the number of free citizens living in Rome at the time – and they reached their seats through rings of arched passages. The arena, below which the wild animals were kept – lions, leopards, bears – before being released for the fight, contained four tunnels and twenty-eight ramps. For special occasions it could be flooded in order to stage massive sea battles.

The fate of prisoners of war and common criminals was in the hands of the crowd. The gladiators, legendarily associated with the words *Morituri te salutant* ('Those about to die salute you'), caused intense excitement in an audience that was intoxicated by such sensational entertainment: applause for the winners, and a humiliating death for the losers, decided by the emperor with a thumbs up.

Left Gladiators fighting wild animals.
Right The façade of the Colosseum, composed of arcades framed with half-columns.
Opposite The cavea, now without its terraces, exposing its substructure and underground passages.
Fold-out The Colosseum, in front of Constantine's Arch. The arcades on the north façade are the best preserved.

A ROMAN CITY IN SPAIN

During the era of the Republic, Rome expanded to the very limits of the Mediterranean (*Mare nostrum*), and signs of Roman settlement can be seen from the Atlantic through to Syria. In Spain, Mérida was the capital of the province of Lusitania, and was founded by Augustus in 25 BC. It was given a theatre – a symbol of Roman culture and urbanization – as well as a neighbouring amphitheatre (AD 87) and aqueducts such as Los Milagros, which is still partially preserved.

At the beginning of the 2nd century, the 'Spanish' emperors Trajan and Hadrian gave the theatre a back wall: the magnificent colonnades of the *scaenae frons* are on two levels. They frame three doors that open on to the *pulpitum* (the stage itself), representing – according to the play that was being performed – the palace, town or country that the actors were supposed to have come from. The doors on the upper storey were reserved for the gods or the emperor. The canopy-shaped kiosks (pairs of columns that punctuate the porticos) housed the statues of donors and public figures on the ground floor, and gods on the first floor. This elaborately decorated back wall became an influential feature of Roman architecture.

In Rome, the theatre changed considerably from its origins in Greece, and eventually became a centre for the *ecclesia* (political community). People in authority had reserved seats, and the emperor made sacrifices there. This state symbolism survives today in many houses of parliament, with their semi-circular seating in which left and right have very specific meanings.

Left Emperor Hadrian, born in Italica in the south of Spain.
Right The two storeys of the *scaenae frons* of Mérida's theatre (2nd century) have been restored and reconstructed.
Opposite The cavea of the theatre, with its two levels of terraces, separated by a gangway. It could hold up to 6,000 spectators.
Fold-out The Roman city of Mérida. To the east of the theatre is the amphitheatre, with a seating capacity of 14,000.

AN AQUEDUCT FOR NÎMES

Water was a major concern for the Romans, allowing their settlements to expand. In order to meet their needs, towns established supply networks that were based on the science of hydraulics. The water was not just for individual consumption, but was also used for ceremonies, swimming pools, public baths and sea-battle circus shows. It was therefore not enough to tap springs and direct the water along simple canals. The Romans also had to learn how to overcome obstacles, use pipes and siphons to cross valleys, find the best way to utilize natural slopes, and devise pressure systems to take the precious liquid across long distances, so that it could power their mills, and fill their public fountains with jets and cascades.

In keeping with traditional worship of nature deities (springs, rivers), the Romans venerated water; aside from their private and public bathhouses, this can be seen in their efforts to construct a massive network of aqueducts, reservoirs, canals both under and above ground, pressurized pipes, and above all the amazing bridges that carried this conquered element, along with distribution tanks and towers to control increases in pressure and attacks from outside.

The Pont du Gard is perhaps the most spectacular of all these constructions. With its length (275 m), its colossal blocks, the perfection of its design, with three sets of superimposed arches 50 m high, its exploitation of the gentlest of slopes in order to carry the water 50 km to Nîmes, this structure – commissioned in 19 BC by Agrippa, the 'right arm of Augustus' – is an absolute masterpiece of technical engineering, built to serve the people of the Roman province of Narbonensis.

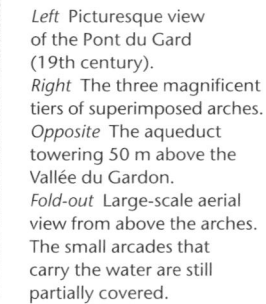

Left Picturesque view of the Pont du Gard (19th century).
Right The three magnificent tiers of superimposed arches.
Opposite The aqueduct towering 50 m above the Vallée du Gardon.
Fold-out Large-scale aerial view from above the arches. The small arcades that carry the water are still partially covered.

THE BEST-PRESERVED ROMAN THEATRE

Aspendos is one of the most important ancient sites in Pamphylia, on the south side of Anatolia. The old city – a walled acropolis on the right bank of the Eurymedon – contained a basilica, an agora, a stadium and several other buildings that have not yet been fully excavated. It also had a very sophisticated system of aqueducts.

The well-preserved cavea of the Roman theatre backs on to the hill. Built in the 2nd century AD by the architect Zenon, the theatre was completed after AD 160, during the reigns of Antoninus and Lucius Verus. It is constructed on a vast scale: 100 m wide, 70 m in depth, with a façade that rises 22 m in a single sweep, it could seat 13,000 spectators. From the colonnaded gallery with its semi-circle of vaulted arches to the back wall of the stage, the building forms a huge shell. The forty rows of seats in the cavea are divided into two levels by a gangway.

The wall of the stage is 50 m wide, decorated with columns on top of which are pediments that are either triangular or round. Behind this is the machinery that allowed actors to appear suddenly on stage – the proverbial *deus ex machina* so beloved of the Greco-Roman theatre. Later, tragedy was replaced by mime, dance, singing competitions, and various bawdy, fantastic or satirical interludes, for during the imperial age the shows became spectacles rather like modern American political conventions. They expressed the political and religious aspects of Roman life, and it was here that offerings were made to the deified emperor, reaffirming the loyalty of Rome's subjects.

Left A performance of a Roman play.
Right The cavea of the theatre, with a colonnaded gallery at the top.
Opposite In the middle of the Pamphylian plain, the acropolis of Aspendos holds many buildings in excellent condition – walls, aqueducts, basilica, temples, stadium and a theatre dug into the side of a hill.
Fold-out The beautifully preserved theatre, completed after AD 160.

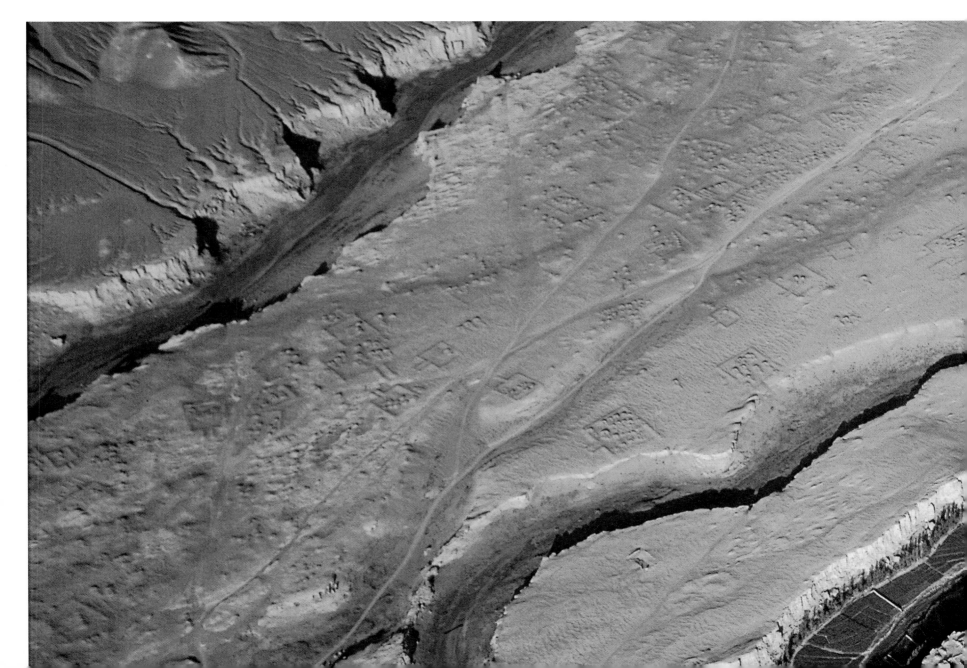

A CITY IN THE FAR WEST OF CHINA

Situated in Xin Jiang, in the west of China, Jiaohe was an outpost in the semi-desert region of Turpan, which in 206 BC was occupied by the western Han. The city was strategically located on the trade route between Asia and the West, and was originally a fortress against invasion by nomadic peoples, then became a stopping-place for caravans, and finally, at the beginning of the modern era, a way station for Buddhism as it moved from India deep into China. This religious propaganda was the work of missionaries such as the monk Xuan Zang, who in the 7th century travelled from China to India and returned with some precious manuscripts. Jiaohe borders on a region where there were flourishing Buddhist monasteries and retreats from an early date – for example, at Baicheng and, further to the east, Dunhuang.

The city nestles between two fertile converging valleys, and is a natural fortress: 650 m long and 300 m wide, it is flanked by rocks up to 30 m in height. Every effort was made to protect this arid promontory from every side: at its narrowest point, the people carved out by hand a massive trench 150 m long and 20 m deep to keep out all attackers.

The Buddhist religion has left a curious monument at Jiaohe: inside a square wall, over which towers a large brick stupa (a dome-shaped Buddhist shrine), there are four groups of twenty-five raised platforms, forming a hundred mounds that are all small stupas. This layout, with two axes crossing at right angles, is emphasized by the central tower, which in turn is surrounded by four small turrets, creating a quincunx. Seen from above, this creates the form of a mandala (a circular diagram representing the universe), symbolizing the mountain of Meru from Indian mythology.

Left Buddhist painting from Dunhuang.
Right One of the Buddhist shrines at Jiaohe is a stupa standing in the middle of four towers, forming a quincunx.
Opposite An aerial view of the stupa, surrounded by one hundred mounds that are divided by cosmic axes.
Fold-out The remains of the city. The Buddhist stupa is on the right.

THE GREAT STUPA TO THE GLORY OF THE BUDDHA

Around the 5th century AD, Indian influence extended as far as Indonesia. Pilgrims were the first to bring Buddhism to the region, and this led to the construction of huge temples. In Java, the biggest of them all – the colossal stupa of Borobudur – was built in around AD 800 in the centre of the island by kings of the Sailendra dynasty, and it marks the apogee of a form of architecture that was designed to be seen by the gods, from above. From ground level it is hard to appreciate the richness of its details or the massive scale on which it is laid out.

This impressive monument is contained within a square (each side measuring 106 m), rising to a height of 35 m. The cruciform ground plan combines elements of the square (representing the earth) and the circle (representing the heavens). It is a typical example of the cosmological representation known as a mandala – a symbolic diagram that illustrates the evolution of the universe from a central point in both Hinduism and Buddhism, and which is used as an aid to meditation.

The structure of Borobudur comprises six square-shaped storeys full of bas-reliefs, surmounted by three concentric circular levels. These contain seventy-two small, open stupas round the central stupa, housing statues of the Buddha seated in the lotus position. The building is designed for the ritual of circumambulation, and on the lower storeys pilgrims can follow scenes in relief from the life of the Buddha in his search for Enlightenment. The sculptures that depict these scenes in various styles cover a total length of 6 km, and mean that the great temple also serves as a visual teaching tool.

Left A scene from the life of the Buddha.
Right Axial view of the terraced base of Borobudur, surmounted by small stupas. The large stupa represents the tomb of the Buddha.
Opposite The fertile plain, at the foot of the Javanese volcano Merapi, is dominated by the temple.
Fold-out Aerial view of Borobudur, allowing the mandala symbolism to be seen in all its glory.

THE GREAT KHMER TEMPLE

The influence of Hindu India spread into south-east Asia, and in Cambodia gave rise to the spectacular monuments of Angkor, capital city of the Khmer Empire. The culmination of this architecture is the great temple of Angkor Wat, dedicated to the god Vishnu and built by King Suryavarman II (r. AD c. 1113–50). The edifice, which is reached via a causeway, is like a large island 1,500 m by 1,300 m, surrounded by a moat 200 m wide. It is laid out in a succession of concentric, rectangular walls with four gates orientated towards the points of the compass.

The monument itself covers an area of 220 m by 180 m, and is surrounded by galleries whose colonnades house historical and religious bas-reliefs. There are towers at each corner, and on the axes there are ornate gates with dancing *apsaras* (celestial nymphs). In the interior, a second wall of porticos (120 m by 100 m) surrounds the huge central square (40 m each side), which is dominated by a quincunx of five mitre-shaped towers, reaching a height of 40 m. This is a veritable cathedral in the jungle, in this case representing Meru, the sacred mountain of Hinduism.

As well as the temple, which covers an area of almost 200 hectares, Angkor Wat boasted a massive hydraulic system which, with the aid of artificial lakes, turned Angkor into a 'rice factory' that produced up to three harvests a year. The wealth from this alone explains the proliferation of great Khmer temples throughout Indo-China between the 10th and 13th centuries. With the reign of Jayavarman VII (r. AD c. 1181–1215), Angkor Wat became exclusively a centre of Buddhist worship, and Buddhism became the national religion of the Khmer.

Left The temple at the time of its discovery.
Right Axial view of the towers of Angkor Wat. The main gate opens out on to a raised causeway lined with nagas (protective serpents).
Opposite Aerial view revealing the succession of walls, dominated by the central block, which symbolizes the cosmic mountain.
Fold-out The temple of Angkor Wat.

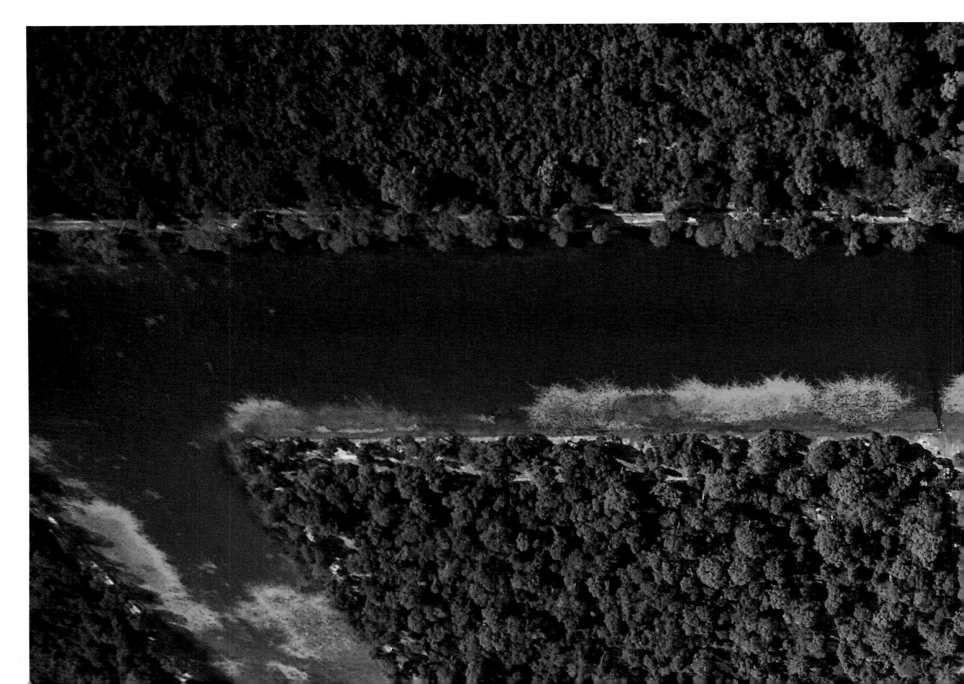

A PRE-COLUMBIAN CITY OF THE GODS

The monuments that the conquistadores discovered in the New World had a long history. The site of Teotihuacán (in central Mexico), which covers an area of 20 km², is on a plateau 2,500 m high, and in the eyes of the Aztecs it already belonged to a mythical age of the immemorial past, when the gods built pyramids to the Sun and Moon. The age of Pre-Columbian Mexico, however, is not as long as that of Europe and Asia, and the ruins of Teotihuacán, the legendary 'City of the Gods', date back to 500 BC at the very earliest.

We do not know the name of the people who built this huge plateau city, which is laid out around the rectilinear Avenue of the Dead, extending over 2 km and lined with monuments such as the citadel and, above all, the two pyramids of the Sun and the Moon. These impressive ruins are on a scale comparable to the pyramids of Giza: the Pyramid of the Sun, the larger of the two, has a base of 225 m by 222 m, and is 65 m high, comprising a staggering 2,500,000 tonnes of material (carried by the workers themselves as there were no carts or beasts of burden). A combination of materials was used: blocks of volcanic stone set in clay were reinforced by internal walls and coated with mortar and stucco.

Teotihuacán was the first capital city of the New World and, with its palaces, sculptures and murals, the fabric of the town continued to expand at right angles to the main avenue. Possibly as a result of invasions from the north, however, the city disappeared around the 6th century AD, after a thousand years of glory.

Left A mask from Teotihuacán.
Right The Plaza of the Pyramid of the Moon, with its platforms and staircases, and the Pyramid of the Sun in the background.
Opposite The massive Pyramid of the Moon, with its stepped façade leading to the top, where priests performed sacrifices.
Fold-out View along the Avenue of the Dead (2 km), with the Pyramid of the Moon and the square in the foreground. On the left is the Pyramid of the Sun.

IN THE HEART OF THE MAYA WORLD

The city of Chichén Itzá was built in Yucatán, a Maya region in the south-east of Mexico. This important cultural centre was then invaded by Toltec tribes from the high plateaux, and as a result it shows both Maya and Toltec influences. Between AD 990 and 1100 their presence brought about a Maya–Toltec renaissance, with the construction of many new buildings. In the Temple of the Warriors we find a fusion of techniques, with Maya stone vaulting and Toltec pillared porticos.

There were also new methods applied to the pyramids: because a form of concrete was used, the angles of the slopes were between 45 degrees and 60 degrees (the angle at Teotihuacán was 30 degrees). The Castillo, also known as the Pyramid of Kukulkan or Quetzalcoatl, which dominates the site, is a good illustration of this evolution: with a square ground plan (55 m each side and 35 m in height), it is divided into nine sections that are decorated with curved motifs reminiscent of Quetzalcoatl, the mythical feathered serpent of Mexico. Each of the four axial staircases contains ninety-one steps (a total of 364), and the threshold at the top, which gives access to the temple, constitutes the 365th step, symbolizing the cycle of the solar year. At the foot of each staircase, the terrible feathered serpents stand guard over the entrance to the sanctuary.

Below this building, archaeologists discovered a well-preserved earlier pyramid, containing a room with a beautiful chacmool sculpture (a man lying on his back, supported by his elbows). This is where the priests would place the hearts of their sacrificial victims.

Left The Maya–Toltec chacmool.
Right The pyramid known as the Castillo, seen from the top of the Temple of the Warriors.
Opposite One of the four great staircases leading up to the temple.
Fold-out The heart of the religious centre of Chichén Itzá: in the foreground, the Temple of the Warriors, surrounded by one thousand columns; in the centre, the pyramid of Kukulkan, crowned by the sanctuary where the sacrifices took place.

29

GUARDIAN OF THE RAINFOREST

When they arrived in South America in 1532, ▓▓▓▓▓ onquista-
dores, led by the adventurer Francisco Pizar▓▓▓▓▓▓elves face
to face with the mighty Inca empire, which ▓▓▓▓nding con-
tinuously since its foundation in 1438. B▓▓▓▓▓ by treachery,
they took the Peruvian monarch Atahu▓▓▓▓r and then executed
him. They entered Cuzco, the capita▓▓▓533. At first there was no
reaction from the empire, which seemed petrified, and it was only later
that there was an attempt at rebellion. The Inca world was a vast, centralized body, based on hierarchical structures and an economic system
that in some ways could be described as socialist: security, forced
labour, distribution of agricultural products, collective ownership.

The empire as a whole fell into the hands of the Spaniards, with the
exception of Machu Picchu, an eagle's nest overlooking the Amazon
jungle, which was not discovered until 1911 by the American explorer
Hiram Bingham. This Inca city lay hidden under the vegetation. It had
never been looted or damaged, and only the thatch and timbers of the
roofs had disappeared. Everything was there: the temples, the houses,
the homes of the chiefs, the priests' sacrificial altars, and even the steep
artificial terraces, known as *andenes*, which demonstrated the Incas'
ingenuity in adapting unproductive land into a source of wealth.

At an altitude of 2,000 m and running for 400 m along the
Urubamba, what was the function of Machu Picchu? The city seems to
have been built as a defensive outpost against attacks from forest tribes,
to deny them access to Cuzco, which was 70 km away as the crow flies.

Left Portrait of the Inca king,
son of the Sun-God.
Right At the top of Machu
Picchu, carved out of solid
rock, is the *intihuatana*,
or 'hitching post of the
sun' – an astronomical
observatory or, rather,
a sacrificial altar.
Opposite The repetitive
layout of homes in
Machu Picchu is a visible
expression of the Incas'
communal system.
Fold-out The Inca city stands
on a mountain terrace
surrounded by steep rocks.

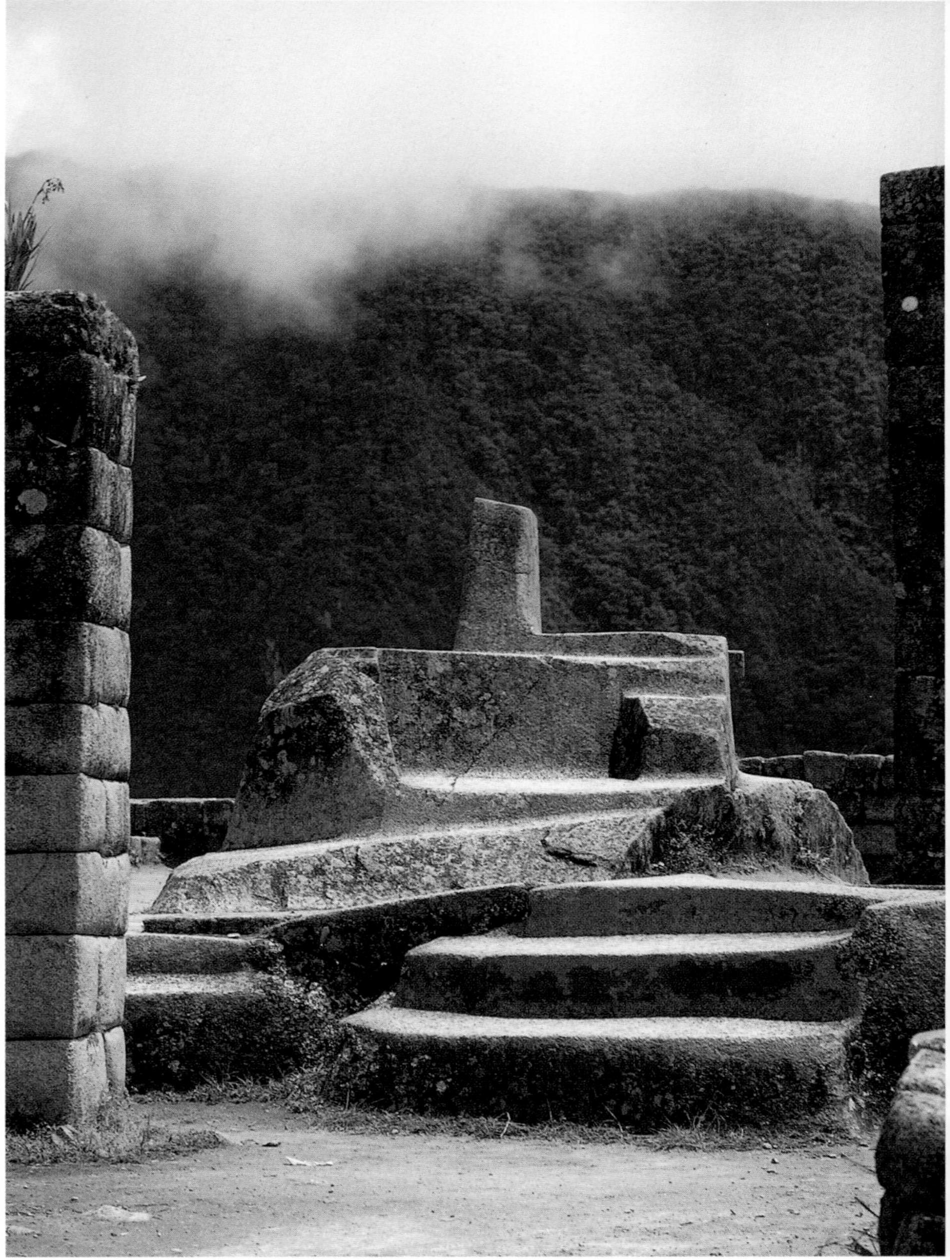

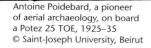

Antoine Poidebard, a pioneer
of aerial archaeology, on board
a Potez 25 TOE, 1925–35
© Saint-Joseph University, Beirut

ILLUSTRATION CREDITS

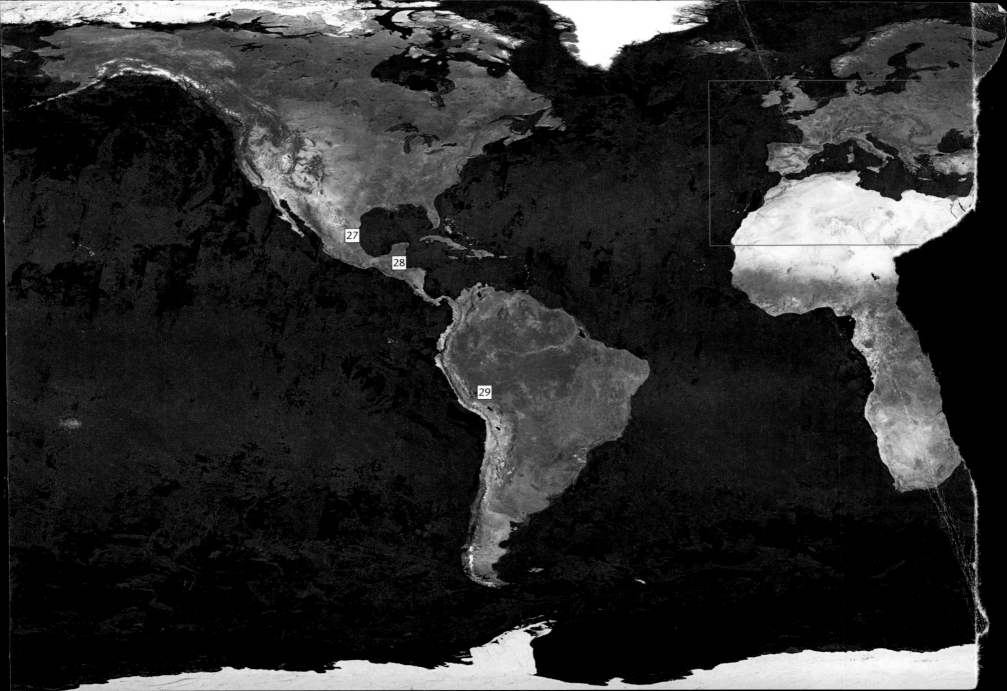

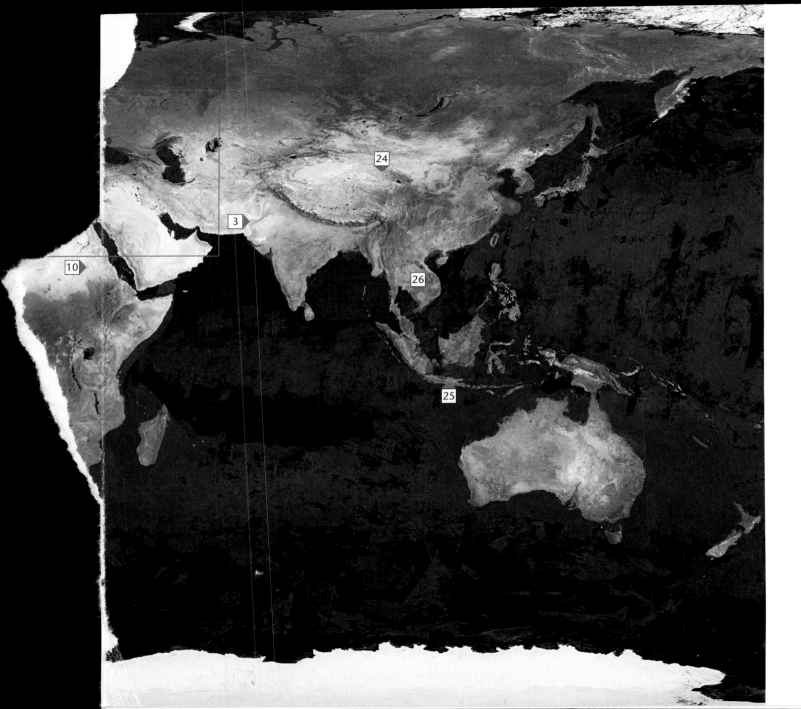

30

1 ▶ MALTA

2 ▶ STONEHENGE

◀ 3 MOHENJO-DARO

4 ▶ UR

5 ▶ EBLA

6 ▶ THE PYRAMIDS OF GIZA

7 ▶ DEIR EL-BAHRI

8 ▶ KARNAK

9 ▶ THE RAMESSEUM

◀ 10 MEROË

11 ▶ MYCENAE

12 ▶ THE ACROPOLIS OF ATHENS

13 ▶ DELOS

14 ▶ PAESTUM

15 ▶ DIDYMA

The
ref
ill

ACKNOWLEDGMENTS

Thanks to Georg Gerster, Kathleen Grosset, Isabelle Lechenet and Patrizia Tardito.

Translated from the French by David H. Wilson

First published in the United Kingdom in 2005 by Thames & Hudson Ltd,
181A High Holborn, London WC1V 7QX

www.thamesandhudson.com

Original edition © 2005 Gallimard Loisirs, Paris
This edition © 2005 Thames & Hudson Ltd, London

British Library Cataloguing-in-Publication Data
A catalogue record for this book is available from the British Library

ISBN-13: 978-0-500-54309-2

ISBN-10: 0-500-54309-7

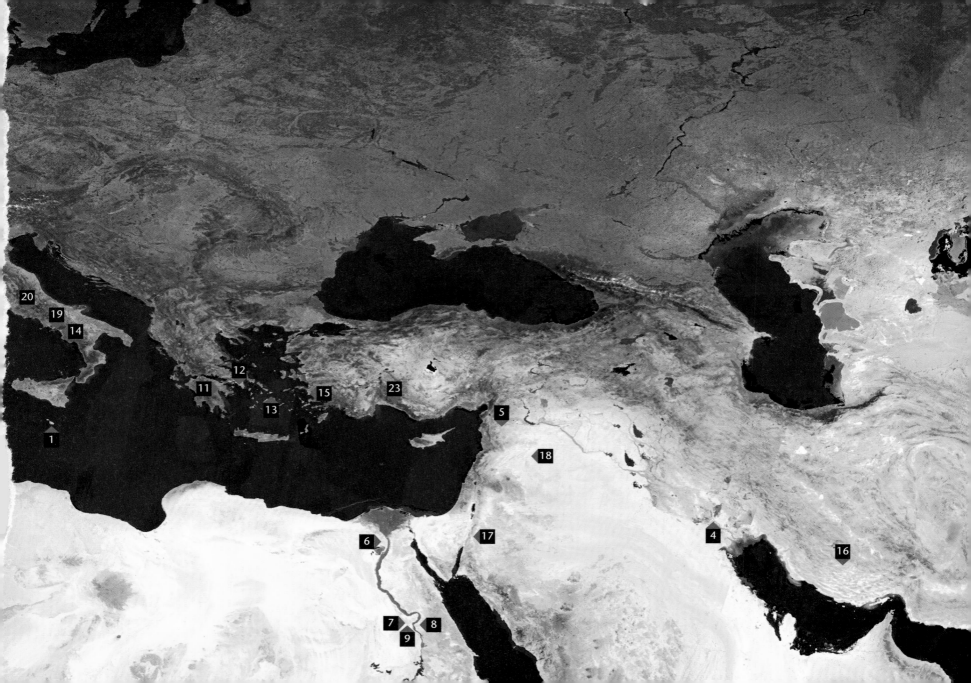

PLANISPHERE